Learning Organization Practices Profile

Guide to Administration and Implementation

Learning Organization Practices Profile

Guide to Administration
and Implementation

Michael J. O'Brien, Ed.D.

An imprint of Jossey-Bass Inc., Publishers

350 Sansome Street, Fifth Floor
San Francisco, CA 94104-1342 USA

ISBN: 0-88390-367-9

Published by
Pfeiffer & Company
An imprint of Jossey-Bass Inc., Publishers
350 Sansome St., 5th Floor
San Francisco, CA 94104
800-274-4434

Table of Contents

Introduction

A new way of managing organizations that is based on the principles of "organizational learning" is spreading throughout the world. This approach is proving to be one of the most advantageous tools an organization can use to adapt to and capitalize on change. Organizational learning results in better bottom lines and improved employee morale.

Executives of organizations, internal and external consultants, and unofficial change agents—the leaders and influencers of organizations—are looking for ways to make their organizations more effective. Many are interested in learning how to operate in a continuous learning mode. The *Learning Organization Practices Profile* (LOPP) and this consulting guide were created in response to this need. They can help you and your organization succeed in a rapidly changing marketplace through continuous and purposeful learning and growth.

The purpose of the *Learning Organization Practices Profile* is to help you to look at the processes and practices of your organization that affect its capacity to learn and change. The information gathered will help you to discover how to make your organization more flexible, more adaptive, and more capable of learning and changing. It provides data that can be used to prioritize organizational-learning goals and develop action plans.

This consulting guide is used in conjunction with the *Learning Organization Practices Profile* (Self-Scored Version). It includes the following information and tools:

* **Journey of a Learning Organization:** The difference between individual and organizational learning; the definition of a learning organization; how learning and changing relate in this context.

* **Purpose and Background of the Profile:** What the LOPP is intended to do and how it was created.

* **Using the Parts To Create a Greater Whole:** Twelve organizational subsystems that affect an organization's ability to operate in a continuous learning mode (the principles and practices of these subsystems are surveyed in the

LOPP). Defines each subsystem and explains its value to the whole system.

* **Ways To Use the Profile:** Specific suggestions for using the *Learning Organization Practices Profile* in organizations whose executives are leading the move toward organizational learning and in those whose executives need to be convinced of the need for change.

* **Administering the Profile:** Suggestions for involving top management, selecting the survey sample, and administering the LOPP.

* **Interpreting the Data:** Step-by-step instructions and worksheets for compiling and interpreting the profile data.

* **What Now? Acting on Profile Results:** Techniques, tips, and a "meeting outline" for using the profile data to stimulate dialogue and develop action plans.

* **References and Further Reading:** A suggested bibliography on the learning organization.

Journey of a Learning Organization

"Learning organization" is not just the new buzzword in organizations that are leaving the Twentieth Century behind. Rather, it is a critical business capability for any organization that wants to survive and prosper in the coming years.

Never before has the rapid increase in new knowledge and technology and in the pace of change itself demanded a learning response as great as what is now required to remain competitive. In real-trade terms, brain power is what matters. Today, individuals and organizations must become continuous learners. It is not surprising to find that the most successful organizations operate in a continuous learning mode.

From Individual to Organizational Learning

To ensure their own and their organizations' success, it is imperative that individuals stay knowledgeable by:

* Assessing their effectiveness with others;

* Keeping their knowledge and skill bases current with the changes in their fields and work processes;

* Looking for on-the-job opportunities to learn new attitudes and new technologies;

* Solving problems creatively; and

* Helping others to learn how to progress through a multitude of changes.

Furthermore, individual learning is no longer enough. Organizational learning must become the standard by which organizations measure their progress. Improvement means change, and, as Ray Stata (1989) writes, "Change is blocked unless all of the major decision makers learn together, come to share beliefs and goals, and are committed to take the actions necessary for change."

In addition to their own learning, individuals—particularly those who lead organizations—must also help their organizations learn to become more flexible and adaptive. They must:

* Find ways to communicate new learnings quickly and effectively;

* Help work teams to take risks and learn from mistakes;

* Utilize computer technology to create "organizational memory"; and

* Build organizational cultures that foster growth.

This is a great challenge, but many organizations are now beginning to embrace the process of continuous learning. Once begun, the process becomes easier.

Definition of a Learning Organization

The first step is to truly understand what is meant by the term "learning organization." A learning organization is not simply a group of individual learners. Nor does it set out to learn just for learning's sake.

> **A learning organization is an organization that has woven a continuous and enhanced capacity to learn, adapt, and change into the fabric of its character. It has values, policies, practices, programs, systems, and structures that support and accelerate organizational learning. Its learning results in changes in the ways in which individuals and the organization operate.**

Organizational learning incorporates individual learning and improvement capacity, but goes beyond individual growth to ensure team and organization-wide dialogues and decisions that result in a smarter, more competitive *system*—a system that can respond to the expanding requirements of globalization, empowerment, and technology.

As David A. Garvin (1993) says, learning organizations have effectively incorporated the following activities into their fabric:

* Systematic problem solving;

* Experimentation with new approaches;

* Learning from their own experiences and history;

* Learning from the experiences and best practices of others; and

• Transferring knowledge quickly and efficiently throughout their organizations.

Learning and Change

A learning organization is one that supports and promotes change, for the processes of learning and changing are inseparable. As Richard Beckhard and Wendy Pritchard (1992) state, "Change is a learning process and learning is a change process."

Learning is the prerequisite to successful change. As organizations strive to adapt to the many changes in the business environment (e.g., rapidly evolving technology, increasing global competition, diminishing natural resources, and a more diverse work force), all have much to learn.

Changes in the marketplace generate organizational responses (including participative management, empowerment, flattening structures, quality initiatives, team work, and more computer technology) that put all of us in unfamiliar territory. We have to learn and adapt as we go along. We need to keep learning what needs to be stopped because it represses learning and creativity and what needs to be started to promote growth and development.

Moreover, the very nature of the learning process that we must go through is fundamentally different from the educational paradigm to which we are accustomed. In the past, as the waves of change rolled slowly, we could rely largely on our standard educational process—supplemented by occasional corporate training programs—to supply us with the necessary skills and knowledge. Although people have always learned informally and on the job, the conscious, continuous, and quick acquisition of new knowledge, skills, and attitudes was not on the agendas of most organizations or individuals.

That, too, must change. As Arie De Geus, head of planning for Royal Dutch/Shell, one of the most effective learning organizations in the world, says, "The ability to learn faster than your competitors may be the only sustainable competitive advantage" in today's business world.

Adaptive Versus Generative Learning

In the 1980s, the motivation behind organizational learning was the need for companies to *adapt* their products, services, and work processes to the changing times and evolving needs of customers. Now, we are recognizing (sometimes painfully) that adaptive learning is only one step on the journey of the learning organization. The next step is *generative learning*.

Generative learning means looking beyond what exists and being creative, anticipating what might happen, what the customer might want. It means not just solving problems but seeking more creative solutions. An executive at a U.S. automotive company illustrated the value of this learning mode when he said of one of his competitors: "They could never have produced the Mazda Miata solely from market research. It required a leap of imagination to see what the customer *might* want" (Senge, 1990b).

Peter Senge, who has done much to promote the concept of the learning organization, says, "The impulse to learn, at its heart, is an impulse to be generative, to expand our capability. That is why leading corporations are focusing on *generative* learning, which is about creating, as well as *adaptive* learning, which is about coping" (Senge, 1990b).

The Concept of Dialogue

Dialogue is a key term in the continuous-learning approach. The basic goal of the process is to create a community of people who are continually in conversation about what they need to learn and how they can learn it. In a learning organization, people meet to create, explore, wonder why, ask "how" and "if," and feel comfortable leaving meetings with questions unanswered but with a commitment to answer them.

Dialogue, as opposed to everyday discussion, is a free-flowing conversation that results in everyone achieving an understanding beyond that of any one individual. Dialogue involves looking at complex ideas from many points of view. Discussions, on the other hand, tend to be conversations about the pros and cons of an already known idea. (See Peter Senge, 1990a, for more on this.) In short, dialogues are for opening, exploring, and discovering. What is created as the result of a dialogue is something new.

Purpose and Background of the Profile

The second stage of the journey of developing organizational-learning capacity involves looking at where an organization is right now in terms of organizational learning principles and practices. Only by identifying the current reality can the organization identify the changes that need to be made and the direction in which it will travel.

The *Learning Organization Practices Profile* is a diagnostic questionnaire that allows managers and human resource professionals to examine twelve subsystems that affect organizational learning (O'Brien & Kremer Bennett, 1994). The profile examines the learning capacity of an organization from the perspective of these twelve subsystems:

* Vision and Strategy
* Executive Practices
* Managerial Practices
* Climate
* Organizational and Job Structure
* Information Flow
* Individual and Team Practices
* Work Processes
* Performance Goals and Feedback
* Training and Education
* Rewards and Recognition
* Individual and Team Development

Purpose of the Profile

The function of the *Learning Organization Practices Profile* is to facilitate a diagnostic process by which an organization can measure its capacity as a learning organization. The purpose of the LOPP is to promote discussion and to help people begin to purposefully explore the issue of organizational learning and development. Use of the LOPP lets the leaders in an organization discuss more intelligently many of the principles and practices required of adaptive organizations.

Once the profile results are compiled, the organization will have an excellent picture of how well its subsystems support continuous learning and which ones provide the best opportunities for improvement.

There is no magic formula to bring about organizational learning; each organization must discover or invent those practices that will work for its unique character. However, the successful practices of other organizations and the principles that form the basis of the *Learning Organization Practices Profile* provide an excellent starting point.

Background of the Profile

The LOPP has been created by studying more than thirty-five, successful, Fortune 1000 corporations, in both the manufacturing and service sectors, that have been purposefully going about the business of becoming adaptive, flexible, learning organizations. These include Analog Devices, Apple, ARCO, AT&T, Bell Atlantic, Con Agra, Corning, Eastman Kodak, Federal Express, General Electric, Honda, Johnsonville Foods, Miles Consumer Healthcare Products, Motorola, NASA, Procter & Gamble, Royal Dutch/Shell, 3M, Wal-Mart, and Xerox. The author learned about the learning practices of these organizations through his consulting work in a number of them and through an extensive review of the literature. An original set of several hundred items was categorized and whittled down by a group of experts in the field of organization development. The results were sorted, then further reduced to a list of one hundred items, which formed the basis of the original profile. That list has been distilled to sixty items for this self-scoring version of the LOPP.

Repeated tests and the opinions of the experts consulted indicate that the items in the LOPP measure what they purport to measure. In May, 1994, The American Society for Training and Development's Learning Organization Network released "Best Practices Study: Sharing Learning in Learning Organizations." The findings of this study, in general, support the usefulness of the categories and items in the LOPP in measuring an organization's learning capacity. Reliability testing is now being done on the LOPP, and a data base is being created that will benefit this new field of study.

Although it is likely that no organization would score high on all the attributes in the profile, deliberately working to incorporate these principles into its system will put any organization well on its way to becoming a learning organization.

Using the Parts To Create a Greater Whole

A Systemic Perspective

It is critical to remember that the phenomenon of the learning organization is based on the principle that the organization is a system—an interconnected whole that "moves and breathes" as one organism. In a system, everything is connected to everything else. Examining the parts of a system allows us to better see the whole. Working on the parts of the system from a systemic perspective synergistically expands each part's influence on the whole organization.

Because of the interconnections between the organization's subsystems, any changes to any part of the overall system have a ripple effect on the other parts. That is, what happens in one part of the organization affects the other parts, or subsystems, of the organization. Therefore, to improve an organization's ability to learn and change, timely adjustments usually need to be made in many of the subsystems, and the commitment and vision from the organization's leaders must be for the whole system in order for any part of it to work effectively.

The *Learning Organization Practices Profile* divides the organizational system into subsystems for three reasons:

1. It helps an organization's leaders and managers understand the many systemic factors that impact the organization's ability to compete successfully in the new world marketplace.

2. It provides an easy tool with which to identify the organization's most critical areas for development.

3. It offers the organization's leadership a vehicle for easily prioritizing goals and steps for action plans.

The following paragraphs describe the twelve subsystems that affect an organization's learning capacity.

Vision and Strategy

An organization must have a clear vision of its goals to ensure that its members—managers and employees—know the direction in which their learning efforts need to be focused. The organization then must develop specific strategies for achieving its vision—strategies that include learning as well as doing.

Without a vision and a commitment to achieving it, as expressed in the strategies, an organization has no goals for any of its other subsystems. Vision and strategy provide the force that drives individuals' motivation for continuous learning and change.

An effective vision in a learning organization is a compelling one that inspires people to act. It includes a commitment to learning and changing as a way of life.

In an interview with Calvin Wick (Wick & Leon, 1993), Ted Hutton of Waverly, Inc., said, "In a company, you must make people understand where you are going so they can anticipate the future. Then, if they believe in it and feel that they have a part in developing your course of action, they are going to work to the best of their ability."

Executive Practices

According to Beckhard and Pritchard (1992), "The most important single instrument for ensuring that learning and change take place is the set of positive and negative rewards that are demonstrated by management behavior. If the stated values and priorities are not consistent with the behavior of the leadership, the change will not stick."

As with any system-wide initiative in an organization, if the leaders do not adhere to the principles and adopt the practices of a learning organization, those whom they lead will not sustain the initiative.

In a learning organization, the behavior of executives models that which they desire of their employees. Executives engage in professional development. They speak often about the connection between continuous learning and organizational results. They visibly lead and facilitate problem-solving efforts and special projects.

Managerial Practices

The practices adopted by managers in a learning organization are a critical component for ensuring the success of that organization. Without managerial practices that support the vision and strategy of a learning organization, the efforts of the rest of the organization will fail.

Managers provide a key link between executives and employees. They must encourage their staffs' learning and development and share the resulting insights, innovations, and new models with the executives, who can learn from that information and change to reflect their new learning. In addition, because managers are the day-to-day interpreters of the organization's vision and strategy, they can directly influence the ways in which the vision, strategy, and resulting business goals are implemented.

In a learning organization, managers support learning by doing. They communicate effectively about their employees' developmental needs and encourage ideas for improvements. They focus on supporting and assisting and they admit their own mistakes. These managers adopt an approach similar to that found at Chaparral Steel, the tenth-largest U.S. steel producer. One reason that Chaparral has set records for productivity and has been rewarded for its high quality standards is its egalitarian management philosophy. Administration Vice President Dennis Beach says, "We manage by adultery. We treat everyone like an adult" (Leonard-Barton, 1992).

Climate

An organization's climate, atmosphere, or culture is another component that plays a critical role in supporting organizational learning. To truly achieve the goals of a learning organization, the climate must allow and reward the kinds of behaviors that promote learning. In learning organizations, people are not afraid to share ideas and speak their minds; the barriers between management and nonmanagement are eliminated; people feel that they are listened to; and individuals support their own and one another's well-being.

One of the key components of a successful learning organization is a climate of openness, in which mistakes are regarded as learning opportunities and people are not afraid of being blamed or punished. In one organization, a department that had a climate of blaming people for problems and mistakes turned the situation around. To help people understand the futility of blaming, the department turned blaming into a game in which a different person was assigned each week to be the scapegoat for every problem, failure, or mistake that occurred that week. Within a short while, people saw how ridiculous and unproductive the blaming was. With this new insight, their willingness to assume responsibility and take risks increased, and more learning and improvement occurred.

A positive climate also affects the bottom line. As Hal Rosenbluth, CEO of Rosenbluth Travel, says, "Each individual has a different dream, and we want dreams to become realities. That's the kind of company we look to be for our people. As a result of that environment, we are able to provide unbelievable levels of service" (Wick and Leon, 1993).

Organizational and Job Structure

The learning organization views itself as an interconnected system. The structure and organization of jobs within the organization must support this systemic view. As a result, in learning organizations, job structures are fluid and evolving. Assignments are frequently rotated; self-directed, cross-functional work teams direct the work processes. Bureaucracy and rules are kept to a minimum.

A classic example of a highly successful company that excels in this area is Johnsonville Foods, the Wisconsin sausage maker that dramatically increased its bottom line when it transformed into a learning organization (Honold, 1991). In this company, "members," rather than "employees," are encouraged to learn every aspect of the business, even those that are traditionally relegated to senior management. Virtually all work is done in teams, including performance reviews and compensation decisions.

Information Flow

Availability of information is critical to the overall success of the learning organization. Without information, people cannot identify what needs to change and, therefore, what they need to learn and do differently. In learning organizations, information systems support the continuous flow of information to all employees. This includes feedback and debriefing to all in the systems.

Advanced organizations use advanced technology, as well as more traditional communications, to improve the flow of information. They allow easy access to organizational and customer information, including financial data.

For example, the amazing success of Wal-Mart is attributed in part to its strategy of using the latest technology to provide up-to-date information to all of its employees and suppliers. Wal-Mart owns its own satellite communication system, which is connected with every point of sale in every store, as well as with every vendor. Every store has access to immediate financial data necessary for decision making, and every vendor has relevant point-of-sale data that allows for cost-effective ordering and inventory control.

At another successful organization, Du Pont Merck, Executive Vice President Kurt Landgraf communicates by voice mail with every one of the organization's 2,200 employees each month to let them know what is going well and what isn't.

Individual and Team Practices

Individuals and the teams in which they operate must be in alignment with the principles and practices of continuous learning in order to ensure success. As a result, learning organizations encourage individuals to continually examine their motives and behaviors with the intention of discovering and remedying their shortcomings. Individuals and teams minimize blame and fear and, in conflict situations, openly and honestly discuss the issues and work toward solutions. People continually seek to learn and grow individually and to share what they've learned with others throughout the organization.

Chaparral Steel is one organization that has made continuous learning and improvement the business of every employee. This firm has empowered every individual to independently identify and solve problems. As a result, as one Chaparral foreman said, "Whoever can come up with an idea on how to fix it, from the millwrights or myself right on up to the top, does it right then. We are all out here to make it run. Probably 90 percent of the problems never even make it to the morning meetings [held to discuss problems]. They are fixed in the field."

Work Processes

People and systems can learn, but if the actual work processes themselves do not support the implementation of new learning, organizational learning breaks down. Therefore, learning organizations design work processes that accomplish the following:

* Incorporate systematic problem-solving techniques;

* Allow for experimentation and new approaches;

* Encourage learning from and sharing with others; and

♦ Promote a systemic view of the organization.

For example, Xerox Corporation, one of the first companies to focus on and reap the rewards of organizational learning, has trained all of its employees in a six-step, problem-solving process that involves creative idea generation, constant questioning, and disciplined thinking. The process is required to be followed at all meetings and is used for making virtually all decisions at Xerox.

Quite simply, learning organizations make learning part of working. As Dorothy Leonard-Barton (1992) writes, "The next frontier for production...is running operations as learning laboratories."

Performance Goals and Feedback

A learning organization focuses on setting goals that meet the needs of its customers. All learning and changing are done in the context of customers' needs so that the organization is learning the things that matter.

As part of its successful effort to meet the challenge of competition for virtually the first time since its founding, Eastman Kodak Company decided that in order to establish goals, it needed to find out what its customers really wanted. To do so, according to Wick and Leon (1993), the company looks at its most demanding customers and then tries to meet their requirements. Individual goals and performance feedback are based on overcoming the gaps to meet those needs, rather than on the activities or functions of a particular task. Without feedback indicating gaps between goals and actual results, performance can stagnate or decline.

Feedback from customers, whether internal or external, is essential to ensuring that the organization's goals and, therefore, its learnings, are focused in the right direction. In learning organizations, feedback is valued and sought after; feedback is the breakfast of champions—although it often contains a lot of fiber. "We look on constructive criticism as a gift from a friend," says Hal Rosenbluth of his highly successful travel company, "and here it's like Christmastime every week. It has to be looked at as a gift from a friend or the company is not going to progress."

Training and Education

In a learning organization, training and education must support the principles of organizational learning. Formal training and educational efforts must focus on helping people to learn from their experiences and those of others, to become more creative and better problem solvers, and to improve their on-the-job performance. Training efforts also must focus on key performance issues and not try to be all things to all people.

One of the leading examples of a successful learning organization is Corning Inc. When Corning was incorporating the principles of continuous learning into every aspect of the organization, its leaders knew that they had to provide training and education that would support their efforts. "Without meaningful education and training to support the ongoing change process, we were not going to keep up," says Ed O'Brien, corporate director of Corning's education, training, and recruiting (Wick & Leon, 1993).

However, Corning also acted on the knowledge that traditional training was no longer sufficient. Training methods such as peers teaching peers, distance learning, technology-based learning, mentoring, coaching, study teams, team training, and demonstration projects are common in learning organizations such as Corning and Xerox.

Rewards and Recognition

The behaviors and types of thinking that an organization recognizes and rewards are what the organization will see in its members. Therefore, this key subsystem must be set up to support the philosophy and practices of organizational learning. In a learning organization, people are recognized and rewarded for continuous learning and change, for taking risks, for developing themselves and others, and for solving problems and meeting challenges. They are not blamed or punished for making mistakes.

In one Wexner retail store, buyers are rated on both their successes and their failures. Too few failures is seen as a sign that the buyer hasn't taken enough risks.

At Wal-Mart, the discount retail chain that is outperforming every other organization in its industry, employees are recognized and rewarded for continuous learning. Among the ways in which Wal-Mart's recognition subsystem backs up its continuous learning philosophy are sharing profits with all of its "associates," providing bonuses for problem solving, and having its executives spend four days of nearly every week visiting and supporting individual stores and their employees.

Individual and Team Development

Learning organizations want their people to grow and develop continually, and effective organizations support this by providing individual- and team-development opportunities on a regular basis. Such organizations structure the work setting so that people learn directly from their work experiences. These organizations support individual and team development through high-quality development plans that include both formal and on-the-job learning opportunities.

At Johnsonville Foods, for example, every employee is given one day a year to spend with an employee in another department in order to learn more about the organization (Honold, 1991).

J.P. Morgan & Co., Inc. is another organization that has used the principles and practices of continuous learning to become one of the most successful banks in the country. One of the key strategies behind its success is its approach to employee development. For example, every job assignment at J.P. Morgan is a "stretch" assignment. "The notion of staffing a position with someone who is fully capable of executing that role is an anathema," says Marion Gislason, head of Morgan's corporate training unit (Wick & Leon, 1993). The result, she says, is the best possible service for the firm's clients.

Ways To Use the Profile

The *Learning Organization Practices Profile* is a powerful vehicle for those with a vision of assisting in the creation of an effective learning organization.

The profile can be used in one of two ways, depending on the internal conditions in your organization. The profile is valuable for achieving either of the following goals:

* To support the strategic direction of an organization whose executive leadership has already decided to follow the path of organizational learning.

* To acquire data for building a case to convince the executive leadership of an organization that it is essential for it to begin to operate in a continuous learning mode.

Depending on the needs of your organization, the profile can be used for measuring and monitoring practices and for gathering data to stimulate dialogue about the organization's vision and strategy. Some ideas for specific ways to use the profile are provided here as a starting point to help you develop the most appropriate uses of the profile for your organization.

Measuring and Monitoring

As a measuring device, the profile can be used in the following ways to accomplish the goal of developing the capacity for organizational learning:

* To assess an organization's current practices to discover how much they support continuous learning;

* To measure improvements or other changes in organizational learning practices over time;

* To systematically identify areas that need the most attention in order to better prioritize needs and assign resources;

* To create a "before" and "after" picture of an organization that is determined to implement the principles and practices of a learning organization.

Data for Planning

As a source of information for dialoguing, discussing, creating a vision, and planning, the *Learning Organization Practices Profile* can be used in the following ways:

- To stimulate dialogue and discussion among the organization's executives about principles and practices of organizational learning and how these might apply to their particular organization;

- To provide an impetus for brainstorming, prioritizing, and action planning for adopting the principles and practices of learning organizations;

- To provide a focus for strategic planning that incorporates the vision and strategy to facilitate a learning organization;

- To provide information about the organization in order to develop action plans related to improving specific processes that affect organizational learning;

- To monitor change and to generate feedback about the organization's continuous-learning practices in order to ensure appropriate adjustments to the plan.

Administering the Profile

When administering the *Learning Organization Practices Profile*, two key points to remember are that it is critical to involve the senior management of the organization and that it is also essential to involve as many and as representative a number of other members of the organization as possible in completing the profile.

Involving Top Management

The best use of the *Learning Organization Practices Profile* is to involve the organization's senior management in the process as soon as possible. Becoming a learning organization is a systemic process that necessitates buy-in and leadership from the executive team.

Setting the Stage for Top Management

As soon as possible, present your plan to the senior-management team (of either the entire organization or of that portion of the organization that is involved in this process), and ask for its involvement. The most reliable data is generated when the profile is completed at the request of senior management, because people pay more attention when the process is important to the executives. Furthermore, when the request is seen as coming from the top, the change process has already begun.

If you are using the profile to gather data to support the development of an organizational-learning strategy, rather than as part of an existing strategy, you may need to discuss with the executives why it is important for them to support this initiative.

Outline the time frame for obtaining and reviewing the data, including what you expect of top management and when. Let the top-management team know what kind of data might be generated. Explain that you will be meeting with the team to review this data and develop action plans. If possible, set the date for that meeting.

Communicating Management Support

All those who will be completing the profile need to know that senior management has a strong interest in the data that the profile will produce.

One way to communicate this support is to send a letter from senior management along with each profile that is sent out to be completed. This letter should emphasize how important it is to the executives that each individual complete the profile and why. Some of the reasons that participation is important are as follows:

- The ability of an organization to learn and do, rather than just do, is the key ingredient for surviving and prospering in today's marketplace.

- The *Learning Organization Practices Profile* will help the organization discover its current organizational-learning practices so that it can progress in this critical business capability.

- Because the survey is designed to look at the organization as a whole system, it is essential that every aspect of that system be examined and that these aspects be viewed from as many perspectives as possible. As a result, every individual's part in completing the profile is important.

- With the data that is gathered, the organization will have the knowledge to begin to use the principles and develop the practices of continuous learning that have resulted in great successes for other organizations and their employees.

- This profile is part of a continuous cycle of 1) using information from every level and function in the organization to identify ways to improve and change; 2) implementing and monitoring that change; 3) making adjustments; and 4) identifying more improvements and other changes.

Selecting the Survey Population

Selecting the survey population is an important step. The goal is to ensure that every perspective, function, and level in the organization is represented. How you achieve this goal depends on the size and makeup of the organization you are surveying.

- **If you are working with a small organization or a small portion of a large organization:** Consider having everyone take the profile. This is the best way to obtain the most complete data. It also provides a significant advantage in that all members of the organization feel that they have had input into the process.

* **If you are working with a large organization:** Use as large a sample as you can compile results for. If you must survey only a portion of the population, make sure you select a representative, cross-sectional, diagonal slice that includes all departments, functions, levels, and so on.

Administering the Survey

Depending on your situation, you can administer the profile either in group meetings or by having individuals complete profile forms on their own and then return them.

Group Meetings

This is the best administration method if your sample population is not too large and if you have the time to set up and conduct group meetings. This method ensures more complete participation of the population sample and establishes a clear understanding of the purpose of the profile.

The following can help to ensure the success of group administration of the LOPP:

* Allow about one hour for the meeting.

* When sending requests for people to attend the meeting, include a cover letter from senior management stressing the importance of the profile.

* Begin the meeting with an introduction to the profile, including why it is being administered in your organization and how the data it generates will be used. Identify the boundaries of the "organization" to be assessed (e.g., entire organization, operating unit, department).

* After the introduction, have people individually complete their profile forms. Be sure to tell people which level of the organization they should be considering as they respond to the items. When they are finished, have them turn in their scoring sheets to you.

* *Optional:* If the time and interest are available, conduct a group-scoring and initial data-interpretation session at the same meeting. Have large scoring sheets prepared in advance (such as on flip-chart pages), and have individuals mark their subsystem and total scores on these sheets. Use the information in the next section ("Interpreting the Data") to facilitate an initial dialogue about the data generated at the meeting.

Administration to Individuals

If your situation is such that the best way to gather data is to send profiles out to individuals to complete and return, do the following:

* Enclose a cover letter from senior management with each profile to ensure that individuals understand the importance of completing the profile.

* In the cover letter, draw the participants' attention to the three levels of the organization from which they will choose at the start of the profile. Tell the participants which organizational level they should be considering when responding to the items, and have them check the appropriate box.

* Set a date by which the scoring sheet must be returned. Make this date clear in the cover letter. Allow a week to ten days, no more, to complete and return the profile.

* Specify the location to which all completed profiles must be sent. If possible, provide each participant with a preaddressed envelope for returning the completed profile.

* If confidentiality is a concern, consider contracting with an outside vendor to process the completed profiles. In that case, have the profiles mailed directly to that vendor.

When all profiles have been returned and the data compiled, use the guidelines in the next section to interpret the data.

Interpreting the Data

Interpretation of the *Learning Organization Practices Profile* tends to be fairly straightforward. Because the profile items are based on the practices of effective learning organizations, the scoring clearly reflects the degree to which the organization follows those practices. You can use the sample worksheets on the following pages to record the compiled data and to begin to develop an interpretation of the profile.

Beyond simply reviewing the current practices of an organization, an interpretation of the results of a group of profiles can be significantly enhanced by asking and answering the following questions:

- How consistent are the individual scores? Do most individuals agree with whether a given practice is used? Is this because of a lack of knowledge about the particular area involved? Is it because the individuals have different criteria for making their assessments? There may be no real answers here, but the purpose is to initiate dialogue, to search for reasons for different perceptions, and to stimulate people to think about the ramifications of the data.

- Are there certain trends across subsystems? For example, are the scores particularly low or high for practices that involve formal systems versus informal communication; for high-level, global thinking versus day-to-day systems and processes; or for an internal focus versus an external one?

- Which categories have the highest scores and which have the lowest? How do these relate to the organization's business results?

- How do the results differ in terms of the demographic data (if any) gathered during the survey? Do the scores differ between management and nonmanagement responses? between functions? between management levels? between different locations within the organization?

A key point to remember—and to communicate to those whose profiles you are interpreting—is that no organizations, not even those who are leaders in the learning-organization movement, achieve a score at or near 100 percent. No organization, however excellent, is perfect.

Nor do the scores imply judgments of "good" or "bad." Rather, the scores simply point out areas in which an organization is strong and areas in which it can focus its improvement efforts. In fact, some low scores are to be expected; it simply means that there are many opportunities for growth and improvement.

Compiling the Results

The steps and worksheets that follow can help you to compile and interpret the data generated by the LOPP.

1. At the top of the "Group Compilation Sheet by Subsystem," record the name of the organization and the number of completed profiles returned.

2. For each subsystem, add up the "final subsystem scores" from all of the returned scoring sheets. Record these totals in column 2 of the Group Compilation Sheet by Subsystem.

3. For each subsystem, determine the "group average score" by dividing the final subsystem score by the number of completed profiles. Record these figures in column 3 of the Group Compilation Sheet by Subsystem.

4. Add the group average scores and enter the total in the box labeled "Total of Group Average Scores." Then divide that total by twelve (the number of subsystems) and record the new figure in the box labeled "This Group's Total Profile Score" on the Group Compilation Sheet by Subsystem.

Group Compilation Sheet by Subsystem

Name of Organization: _____

No. Profiles Returned: _____

1. Profile Subsystem	2. Final Subsystem Score	3. Group Average Score
A. Vision and Strategy		
B. Executive Practices		
C. Managerial Practices		
D. Climate		
E. Organizational and Job Structure		

1. Profile Subsystem	2. Final Subsystem Score	3. Group Average Score
F. Information Flow		
G. Individual and Team Practices		
H. Work Processes		
I. Performance Goals and Feedback		
J. Training and Education		
K. Rewards and Recognition		
L. Individual and Team Development		

Total of Group Average Scores:	
This Group's Total Profile Score:	

5. To get a picture of the group's response pattern, plot its average subsystem scores on a diagram such as the one below titled "Average Scores for Subsystems." To do so, mark where the group average score for each subsystem falls on the diagram and either connect the scores to create a line graph or shade in the spaces to make a bar chart.

Average Scores for Subsystems

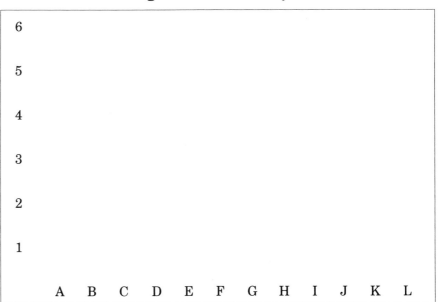

6. The twelve subsystems can be divided into three categories as another way of examining the organization systemically. You may want to determine the average scores for each category. To do so, complete the following steps:

- First, transfer the group average scores for all the subsystems to the "Group Compilation Sheet by Category," which follows. Record those numbers in the spaces next to the subsystem name in column 1 of the worksheet, "Group Average Scores per Subsystem."

- Next, for each category, add up the four group average scores. Record this total in column 2, "Total Group Category Score."

- Divide each total group category score by four (the number of subsystems per category). The result is the "Average Category Score." Record this number in column 3 of the worksheet.

Group Compilation Sheet by Category

Name of Organization: _____

1. Group Average Scores per Subsystem	2. Total Group Category Score	3. Average Category Score
Leadership:		
A. Vision and Strategy _____		
B. Executive Practices _____		
C. Managerial Practices _____		
D. Climate _____		
Job Structure and Systems:		
E. Organizational and Job Structure _____		
F. Information Flow _____		
G. Individual and Team Practices _____		
H. Work Processes _____		
Performance and Development:		
I. Performance Goals and Feedback _____		
J. Training and Education _____		
K. Rewards and Recognition _____		
L. Individual and Team Development _____		

7. If you want to graph the data for each of the three major categories of subsystems, use the following chart.

Average Scores for Major Categories

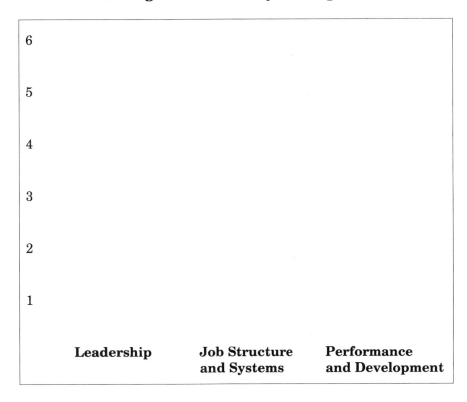

	Leadership	Job Structure and Systems	Performance and Development
6			
5			
4			
3			
2			
1			

8. Identify the three or four highest-scoring and lowest-scoring *subsystems*. You can use the chart below to record them:

Lowest-Scoring Subsystems	Highest-Scoring Subsystems

9. Identify the three or four highest-scoring and lowest-scoring *profile items*. You can use the chart below to record them:

Lowest-Scoring Items	Highest-Scoring Items

10. Extract any other data you wish. For example, you might want to determine average scores for certain demographic groups, such as managers and nonmanagers.

What Now? Acting on Profile Results

The purpose of the *Learning Organization Practices Profile* is to promote dialogue within an organization, from the top down, thereby stimulating the generation of new ideas and action plans for developing the organization's capacity to learn and improve. Therefore, a critical component of administering the profile is the feedback and action-planning meeting with the organization's executive team to examine the profile results and determine the next steps.

Feedback and Action-Planning Meeting

This section contains a suggested outline for a feedback and action-planning meeting, as well as suggestions for starting an action-planning process. This is only a starting point. The profile results will reveal key organizational issues that will require a series of meetings and the development and monitoring of action plans. Use these suggestions as a starting point and adapt them to your particular organization and its issues.

Meeting Goal

The goal of the feedback and action-planning meeting is to produce the start of a broad plan of action as a result of the profile data. It is designed to stimulate dialogue based on the profile data and to identify, at a minimum, the key next steps the organization needs to take.

Meeting Participants

Participants in the first feedback and action-planning meeting should include the senior executives of the organization (or of the portion of the organization that is participating in this initiative). Because the top managers of an organization are responsible for creating and communicating the vision and strategy of the organization, they need to examine the data first and identify where to begin to incorporate organizational-learning principles and practices into the organization.

Once the initial feedback and action-planning meeting with the executive team has occurred, similar meetings should be held throughout the organization to present the profile data and to generate feedback and more ideas. The information coming out of these meetings can then be fed back to the executive team for further consideration and action planning.

Time Required	The initial meeting should take a minimum of two to three hours. Another meeting should be held soon after the first meeting, if necessary, to develop a useful action plan.

Meeting Preparation	Before the initial meeting, prepare a display of the compiled profile data. The display should be geared to meet the needs and interests of the group. Depending on these needs and interests, you can use or adapt one of the following suggested ways of displaying the data:

- If the audience is interested in full data about each of the twelve organizational subsystems, display the average score for each subsystem, as well as the highest and lowest scores and any other relevant statistical data.

- If the audience is interested in less specific data, you can group the twelve subsystems into their three categories and display only the category scoring data.

- If the group is interested only in the highest and lowest scores, you may want to show only the two or three highest-scoring and lowest-scoring subsystems.

Meeting Outline	Before the meeting, prepare an outline that you can use to guide the discussion toward the goal of the meeting. The following is an outline that you can use or adapt for this purpose. Use the information in this booklet to help present ideas and to stimulate dialogue and brainstorming.

1. Present the goal and agenda for the meeting and gain the participants' agreement to follow the agenda.

2. Briefly define and describe a "learning organization." Provide whatever background is important for all participants to understand what a learning organization is. Make it clear that their ability to successfully manage the organization in the future is based, in large part, on the degree to which the organization incorporates the principles and practices of continuous learning.

3. Provide a brief background of the *Learning Organization Practices Profile* and explain how it has been used to gather data for the organization.

4. Present the profile data and explain what the scores and trends mean. Use the guidelines from the previous section of this guide ("Interpreting the Data") to present various perspectives on the profile data: highest and lowest scores,

trends across subsystems or by demographic groups, and so on.

5. Emphasize that there are no good or bad profile scores, simply valuable information that can be used to more effectively manage the organization. Note that this meeting is part of the process of creating an organizational-learning culture in which people do not blame the past but look at where they are in the present and determine what they can do now and in the future.

6. Define the term "dialogue," as it is used in a learning organization (see chapter one, "Journey of a Learning Organization"). Dialogue means looking at complex ideas from many viewpoints, with open minds. "Discussion" often examines the pros and cons of an already-identified issue, whereas the objective of dialogue is to open up, explore, and discover something new. Dialogue is based on the concept of synergy, in which the outcome of people working in concert exceeds what the sum of their outcomes would be if they were working independently. Emphasize that the purpose of dialogue is to wonder, ask, explore, and create, and that it is all right to leave meetings with questions unanswered but with a commitment to answer them.

7. As you facilitate the meeting, model this approach. Stay in a mode of openness, exploration, and discovery. Avoid blaming, judging, or saying that any statement or idea is wrong. Keep your style open and flexible, and encourage the participants to do so, too.

8. Facilitate a dialogue among the participants to begin determining what the data from the *Learning Organization Practices Profile* mean to the organization and how the knowledge gained from the data can be used. This is the key approach to this meeting, because the basic goal of the process is to create a community of people who are continually in conversation about what they need to learn and how they can learn it.

9. Some useful questions to begin the dialogue include the following:

   • Why are our weak areas weak? What are the organization's problems, challenges, and opportunities? Which specific practices (profile items) are of most concern to us?

   • Why are our strong areas strong? What systems and processes are working well and why are they?

- Which subsystems or categories are most critical to achieving our vision of success?

- Which subsystems or categories are holding us back the most?

- How do we, as managers, disagree about our strengths and weaknesses, and why is that?

10. Another way to stimulate dialogue is through a "group mapping" of some of the key profile data. The technique is to have the meeting participants move to locations in the room that represent their opinions of the data, so that people can identify who has similar and who has different opinions in order to engage in dialogue. This activity is particularly effective with a large number of participants.

    The activity can be focused on the two or three biggest challenges or problems. After identifying those issues, go through the following steps for each one:

    a. Have each participant measure his or her awareness of the issue and his or her opinion of its impact on the organization. You can use a worksheet such as the one that follows to have participants graph their positions. Use a separate worksheet for each issue.

    b. The vertical axis measures each individual's personal awareness of the issue as a problem. Ask individuals to indicate how much of a problem they believe this issue to be by rating it on a scale of 1 to 7 (1 = not much of a problem; 7 = a significant problem).

    c. The horizontal axis measures the issue's impact on the organization's effectiveness. Ask participants to rate, on a scale of 1 to 7, how much of a negative impact they believe the issue has on the organization's productivity or effectiveness (1 = not much negative impact; 7 = significant negative impact).

    d. Replicate this seven-point graph using two walls in the back of the room. Have one wall be the vertical axis and the other wall be the horizontal axis. The "graph" is the floor. Hang numbers from one to seven at even intervals on both walls, to indicate the major rating points.

    e. Have the participants move to the spaces on the floor that represent their positions on the individual graph.

f. The participants will end up in clusters on the graph. Have each cluster of individuals begin to talk as a group about why the members rated the issue as they did and what the organization should do about the issue.

11. Using the information that emerges in the dialogue, lead a brainstorming session to generate ideas on how the organization can increase its capacity for learning. One effective way to structure the brainstorming is to have participants generate ideas in the following categories:

   ♦ How fragmentation of thinking, processes, and functions can be changed to a more systemic, unified approach;

   ♦ How competition between individuals and organizational units can be changed to sharing of knowledge and collaboration;

   ♦ How the organization can move from "reactive" problem solving and action to learning and "proactive" action;

   ♦ Other mental models or "mindsets" that exist in the organization that should be questioned or examined;

   ♦ Practices we should stop;

   ♦ Practices we should start;

   ♦ Practices we should continue and enhance.

   List all ideas without comment or evaluation. When the participants have run out of ideas, combine similar ideas. Then evaluate the ideas to provide a list of "workable" suggestions.

12. Based on the results of the brainstorming, have the group begin to develop an action plan for putting to use the common knowledge it acquired as a result of the profile data and the meeting.

   The following are some guidelines for action planning:

   ♦ Prioritize the most important practices to begin work on.

   ♦ Identify the individual or team accountable for each one.

   ♦ Establish a time frame (e.g., three months, six months, a year, two years).

   ♦ Identify any resources and management support needed.

   ♦ Identify any initial obstacles and ways to overcome those obstacles.

13. Set the date and time for the next meeting.

Group Mapping Exercise Worksheet

Issue: _____

Instructions:

1. For the issue named above, determine on a scale of 1 to 7 how much you personally believe this to be a problem (1 = not much of a problem; 7 = a significant problem). Mark this point on the *vertical* axis of the graph below.

2. Next, determine on a scale of 1 to 7 how much of a negative impact this issue has on the organization's productivity or effectiveness (1 = not much negative impact; 7 = significant negative impact). Identify your opinion of the issue's impact separately from your opinion of how big a problem you think it is. When you have determined your rating of this issue's impact, mark the corresponding point on the *horizontal* axis of the graph below.

3. Find the intersection point of your two ratings on the graph and place a mark at this point on the graph.

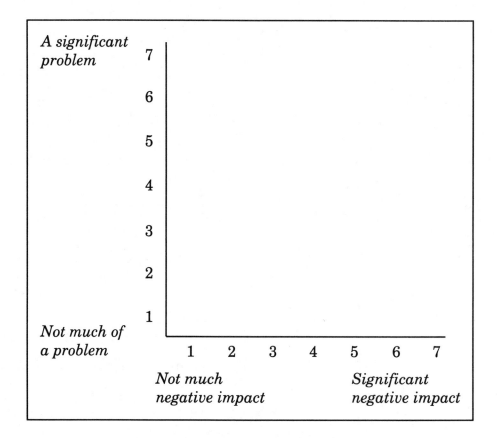

One Company's Example

The following is a summary of how one organization used the *Learning Organization Practices Profile* to enhance its capacity for continuous learning.

The initiative was from senior management, which had made a strong commitment to turn the company into a learning organization. The LOPP was administered to 20 percent, or 200, of the 1,000 employees. Personnel at every level and in every function and location of the organization were included in the survey sample.

The results of the survey were presented at a half-day feedback and action-planning meeting of senior executives. The members of this team were encouraged to be open and in a discovery mode so that new ideas would result. By the end of the meeting, the management team had drafted an initial action plan that included the following major points:

Practices to be implemented immediately:

* The president will speak about the concept of the learning organization at every opportunity.

* Sales representatives will informally obtain customer feedback about one of the organization's newest services.

* The senior vice-president for human resources will include learning-organization information in the monthly company newsletter.

* Each member of senior management will converse regularly with employees throughout the organization to find out from them what senior management is doing to help and hinder the employees.

Issues for immediate action planning:

* A task force will be established to look at changing the reward system to honor employees who take risks and to reward team work.

* Three specific subsystems are identified as the top priorities for change: vision and strategy, management practices, and information flow. Each subsystem is assigned to a member of the executive team. Before the next meeting, the three members are to create a plan to identify and implement the changes needed.

Longer-term goals:

The following are longer-term goals:

* Revise the performance planning and review system to be more customer focused;

* Form cross-functional, self-directed teams to work on key projects;

* Implement a top-down training program on managing change and learning.

Planning for these will be done at future executive meetings.

The executives also decided to share the data from the *Learning Organization Practices Profile* with every employee through a series of feedback and action-planning meetings similar to the one they had just completed.

In those meetings, employees were asked to dialogue and brainstorm ideas, just as the senior managers had done. The meetings were used as opportunities to collect even more data about what could be done and by whom. The feedback and action plans that were generated in these meetings were sent to the executive team, which used the additional information to further modify and expand its action plans and strategies.

References and Further Readings

References

Beckhard, R., & Pritchard, W. (1992). *Changing the essence: The art of creating & leading fundamental change in organizations.* San Francisco, CA: Jossey-Bass.

Garvin, D.A. (1993, July-August). Building a learning organization. *Harvard Business Review,* pp. 78-91.

Honold, L. (1991, April). The power of learning at Johnsonville Foods. *Training,* pp. 55-58.

Leonard-Barton, D. (1992, Fall). The factory as a learning laboratory. *Sloan Management Review,* pp. 23-38.

O'Brien, M., & Kremer Bennett, J. (1994, June). The 12 building blocks of the learning organization. *Training,* pp. 41-49.

Senge, P.M. (1990a). *The fifth discipline: The art and practice of the learning organization.* New York: Doubleday.

Senge, P.M. (1990b, Fall). The leader's new work: Building learning organizations. *Sloan Management Review,* pp. 7-23.

Stata, R. (1989, Spring). Organizational learning—The key to management innovation. *Sloan Management Review,* pp. 63-74.

Wick, C.W., & Leon, L.S. (1993). *The learning edge: How smart managers and smart companies stay ahead.* New York: McGraw-Hill.

Further Readings

Hayes, R.H., Wheelwright, S.C., & Clark, K.B. (1988). *Dynamic manufacturing: Creating the learning organization.* New York: The Free Press.

Kline, P., & Saunders, B. (1993). *Ten steps to a learning organization.* Arlington, VA: Great Ocean/San Diego, CA: Pfeiffer & Company.

Kofman, F., & Senge, P.M. (1993, Autumn). Communities of commitment: The heart of learning organizations. *Organizational Dynamics,* pp. 5-23.

Marquardt, M., & Reynolds, A. (1994). *The global learning organization: Gaining competitive advantage through continuous learning.* Burr Ridge, IL: Irwin Professional Publishing.

Pedler, M., Burgoyne, J., & Boydell, T. (1991). *The learning company: A strategy for sustainable development.* New York: McGraw-Hill.

Savage, C. (1990). *Fifth generation management: Integrating enterprises through human networking.* Burlington, MA: Digital Press/Englewood Cliffs, NJ: Prentice Hall.

Schein, E.H. (1993, Winter). How can organizations learn faster? The challenge of entering the green room. *Sloan Management Review,* pp. 85-92.

Senge, P. (1993). The art & practice of the learning organization. In M. Ray & A. Rinzler (Eds.), *The new paradigm in business: Emerging strategies for leadership and organizational change.* New York: Tarcher/Perigee and World Business Academy.

Short, R. (1991). *A special kind of leadership: The key to learning organizations.* Seattle, WA: The Leadership Group.

Stalk, G., Evans, P., & Shulman, L.E. (1992, March-April). Competing on capabilities: The new rules of corporate strategy. *Harvard Business Review,* pp. 57-69.

Watkins, K.E., & Marsick, V.J. (1993). *Sculpting the learning organization: Lessons in the art and science of systemic change.* San Francisco, CA: Jossey-Bass.

Editor: Arlette Ballew

Production Editor: Dawn Kilgore

Interior Design and Page Composition: Judy Whalen

Cover Design: Paul Bond

This product was edited and formatted using 486 PC platforms with 8MB RAM and high resolution, dual-page monitors. The copy was produced using WordPerfect software; pages were composed with Corel Ventura Publisher software and cover created with CorelDraw software. The text is set in twelve on fourteen New Century Schoolbook and the heads are set in Kabel bold and normal. Proof copies were printed on a 400-dpi laser printer and final camera-ready output on a 1200-dpi laser imagesetter by Pfeiffer & Company.